Saffron Alexander

# The Hidden
# Jewels of London

**DELTA** Publishing

Access all the accompanying digital components for this book on **allango**, the DELTA Publishing language learning platform:

| Scan the QR code or go directly to **www.allango.co.uk** | Search for the title or the ISBN and click on the cover image | Access content, use now or save for later |
| --- | --- | --- |

When you see this symbol, accompanying digital content is available.

**Photos:**
4 123RF.com (aninata), Nidderau; **5** 123RF.com (aninata), Nidderau; **9** 123RF.com (floralset), Nidderau; **83** 123RF.com (iulika1), Nidderau; **84** 123RF.com (norrie3699), Nidderau

1st edition      1  ⁶ ⁵ ⁴ ³ ² | 2027  26  25  24  23

Delta Publishing, 2022
www.deltapublishing.co.uk

© Ernst Klett Sprachen GmbH, Rotebühlstraße 77, 70178 Stuttgart, 2022

Author: Saffron Alexander
Editor: Kate Baade
Cover and layout: Andreas Drabarek
Illustrations: Alice Larsson, Beehive Illustrations
Design: Datagroup int, Timisoara
Cover picture: Alice Larsson, Beehive Illustrations
Printing and binding: Plump Druck & Medien GmbH, Rheinbreitbach

Printed in Germany
ISBN 978-3-12-501148-9

# Contents

# Abbreviations

sb    somebody
sth   something

# Before you start

1. How many tourist attractions in London can you name?

2. Amelia and William know a lot about the history of London. Write down three things about the history of your country.

> Three things about the history of my country
> 1.
> 2.
> 3.

3. Look quickly at the illustrations in the book of Amelia and William. Write down some words to describe them.

| Amelia | William |
| --- | --- |
|  |  |

4. Read the story. Were your ideas about Amelia and William correct?

# Chapter 1

Amelia pulled a book off the bookshelf and flicked through its pages. It was the first day of the summer holidays and she was looking for a good mystery book to read. Amelia loved reading mystery books. When she grew up, she wanted to be a famous detective like Sherlock Holmes or Nancy Drew.

Amelia knew that she would make a great detective when she was older because she was very good at solving clues and puzzles. Every morning, Amelia's father would give her the puzzle section from his newspaper and time how long it took her to solve the clues. That morning, Amelia had solved the puzzle in less than ten minutes. It was a personal best.

Amelia put the book back onto the shelf and continued looking.

"Found anything yet?" a voice asked.

Amelia jumped and turned around. Her friend William was standing behind her, holding a thick book.

---

18 **to flick** to move quickly – 20 **mystery** sth that is difficult to understand or explain –
21 **famous** known by many people – 22 **detective** sb who solves mysteries

"You scared me!" Amelia laughed.

"Sorry," said William. He grinned at her and held the book up for her to see. It was a book all about London parks. Amelia fought the urge to roll her eyes. While she loved reading mysteries, William loved reading non-fiction books about anything and everything. Sometimes, Amelia joked that he was a walking encyclopedia.

"I've been looking for this one for ages!" William said excitedly. "It's got a whole extra section about the history of Green Park! Isn't that brilliant?"

"Um," said Amelia. "If you say so."

"Have you found something to read?" asked William.

"Not yet," said Amelia. She turned her attention back to the bookshelf. "I'm still look–" Amelia froze. Something had caught her eye. There was a book at the end of the shelf, but it did not look like the other books on the shelf. The other books looked new and each one had a sticker on the spine that showed that it belonged to the library. The book that caught Amelia's eye did not look new. In fact, it looked extremely old.

Amelia reached out and pulled the book from the shelf. Unlike the other books on the shelf, it was not a mystery novel. It was an old book all about the history and construction of Tower Bridge. Amelia rolled her eyes.

"You'd probably like this one," she said to William.

"Ooh, yes!" said William. "Can I see it?"

As Amelia held the book up for William to take, something yellow slipped from its pages and fell to the floor.

"What's this?" Amelia asked. She knelt and picked up an old, yellow piece of folded paper. Amelia unfolded the paper and gasped. On it, was a message.

"William!" Amelia whispered excitedly. "Look at this!"

William looked over her shoulder as Amelia read aloud:

---

4 **urge** a strong desire or impulse – 7 **encyclopedia** a book that gives information about many things – 17 **spine** part of a book that shows the title and author's name – 22 **construction** the building of sth

---

> Greetings, dear friend, and good luck to you,
> What you must do is solve my clues...
> Do as I say and follow my rules,
> And you will be rewarded with plenty of jewels.

William looked confused. "What does that mean?"

Amelia did not respond. She was too busy reading what was under the message:

> Clue #1: Step 201.

"Amelia?" William shook her shoulders. "What's going on?"

Amelia did not answer again. Something had suddenly *clicked* in her mind.

"William," she said. "How many steps are in the towers of Tower Bridge?"

"How many steps?" William repeated.

"Quickly!" Amelia hissed. She had a theory, and she wanted to see if she was right.

"Um, I remember I read a story in the news about Tower Bridge before," said William. "I think there are 200 steps in each tower."

Amelia's face fell. "Oh."

"Wait, wait," said William. "Actually, I remember now. There are exactly 206 steps in each tower!"

Amelia waved the piece of paper in front of William's face. "William, I think this is a *clue*."

"A clue?"

"Yes! Don't you see? Someone has hidden some jewels somewhere in London and they want us to find them! I think the

---

21 **theory** an idea about sth

next clue is in Tower Bridge, that's why they hid the note inside this book!"

William did not look convinced.

"Look," said Amelia. "Let's just go and see. We don't have anything else to do today, do we? And Tower Bridge isn't very far from here. It won't take long."

"Fine," said William with a sigh. "But then we're coming straight back to the library."

"Deal," said Amelia with a wide grin. "Let's go!"

As they ran out of the library, Amelia nearly bumped into a tall man wearing a long, black trench coat.

"Sorry!" Amelia yelled, but she did not turn around. If she had, she would have seen the strange look the man gave her.

> What kind of books does Amelia like to read?

> What kind of books does William like to read?

## Think about it...

Amelia thinks non-fiction books are boring. Do you agree with her?

What would you do if you found a secret message inside a book?

---

3 **to convince** to believe in sth – 12 **to yell** to shout

# Chapter 2

Tower Bridge was filled with tourists. Amelia and William waited patiently at the queue by the ticket office.

"Are you sure you want to do this?" William asked.

Amelia rolled her eyes. William had asked her the same question no less than eight times on their journey to Tower Bridge.

"Yes, William," she said. "Don't you want to know if my hunch is right?"

"Not really," mumbled William but Amelia pretended like she didn't hear him.

"I wonder what we're going to find there," Amelia said.

"The treasure?" William suggested.

"Probably not yet," said Amelia. "It'll most likely be another clue."

"Yay," said William dryly. "This wild goose chase continues."

"Where's your sense of adventure, William?" Amelia asked.

---

18 **queue** line – 23 **hunch** guess – 31 **wild good chase** a search for sth unlikely to be real –
32 **sense** a feeling of sth

"Back at the library, in the adventure section."

They waited in the queue for another ten minutes before it was their turn.

"Hello and welcome to Tower Bridge," said the ticket attendant. "How can I help you?"

"Two tickets please," said Amelia. She handed the ticket attendant some of the money her parents had given her at the start of the summer holidays. She had been planning on saving it all to buy a new video game console in a few weeks, but this was more important.

"I'll be taking this from your share of the treasure," Amelia told William as she handed him his ticket.

"If there even is a treasure," said William.

Amelia ignored him and ran ahead. She had seen pictures of the bridge and the two towers before, but she had never seen it up close. It was magnificent. As Amelia pushed through the crowds of tourists, with William trailing closely behind, she couldn't help but feel very impressed.

There was a long queue for a lift to take the tourists up to the top of the tower, but Amelia ignored it and headed for the staircase.

"Why can't we take the lift?" William panted as he ran after her.

"Ssh, William!" Amelia yelled. "You're distracting me. …*eight, nine, 10…*"

"…*199, 200, 201*!" Amelia stood on the 201$^{st}$ step and pumped her arms into the air. "We made it!" She looked over her shoulder but William wasn't there.

"William?" Amelia took a few steps backwards and peered around the winding corner. She still couldn't see William, but she could hear him slowly huffing and puffing up the stairs.

Satisfied that he'd eventually arrive, Amelia hopped back over to the 201$^{st}$ step and peered around. It was grey and made out of

---

6 **ticket attendant** sb who gives out tickets – 9 **video game console** a machine to play video games on – 16 **magnificent** amazing and beautiful – 17 **to trail** to follow

stone just like all 200 of the other steps. Amelia crouched down and looked at it perfectly. There was nothing special about it. No hidden markings, no secret button to press – *nothing*! It was a perfectly ordinary step.

5     "Oh no," Amelia said.

    "Don't say that," William wheezed as he finally turned the corner. He was out of breath from climbing the stairs. "Please don't say *oh no*."

    "We're in the wrong tower," Amelia groaned.

10     "Or there's just no clue," William muttered. "Have you ever considered that?"

    "Do you have to be so negative all the time?" Amelia asked. "Now come on, we have to check the other tower!"

    She patted William gently on the shoulder then began
15 sprinting down the stairs.

    "I'll race you!"

    Amelia and William raced back down the stairs and ran across the glass floor bridge that connected the two towers. If they hadn't been on such an urgent mission to find the next clue,
20 Amelia would have stopped to admire the view on the bridge. In every direction she turned, Amelia could see the city of London glowing under the summer sun. Below them, the waves of the River Thames crashed against the base of the tower. It was beautiful.

25     "Come on, William!" Amelia called. She glanced over her shoulder. William was still lagging behind. "I'll race you to the top of the next tow –"

    Amelia stopped in her tracks.

    She had reached the end of the glass floor bridge but there
30 was a black and yellow rope across the doorway that led to the next tower. Next to the rope, there was a large sign that read:

---

1 **crouched down** to bend down at the knees – 6 **to wheeze** to say sth out of breath –
19 **urgent** very important – 20 **to admire** *(here)* to really enjoy sth – 25 **to glance** to look
quickly – 26 **to lag behind** to fall behind – 28 **to stop in your tracks** to stop immediately

*EAST TOWER CLOSED FOR* MAINTENANCE. *APOLOGIES FOR ANY* INCONVENIENCE.

"Well, I guess that's the end of that," panted William. He was standing crouched over with his hands on his knees, trying his best to breathe. "Can we go back to the library now?"

Amelia thought about it for a few seconds and then shook her head.

"Absolutely not!" Amelia turned to William and grinned. "We're going to sneak in!"

What did Amelia want to do with her holiday money?

Who is fitter? William or Amelia?

## Think about it...

What was the last hunch you had? Were you right?

Amelia wants to sneak into the other tower. Do you think this is a good idea?

---

1 **maintenance** important work – 1 **apologies** a formal way of saying sorry –
2 **inconvenience** trouble – 9 **to sneak in** to go in without anybody seeing

# Chapter 3

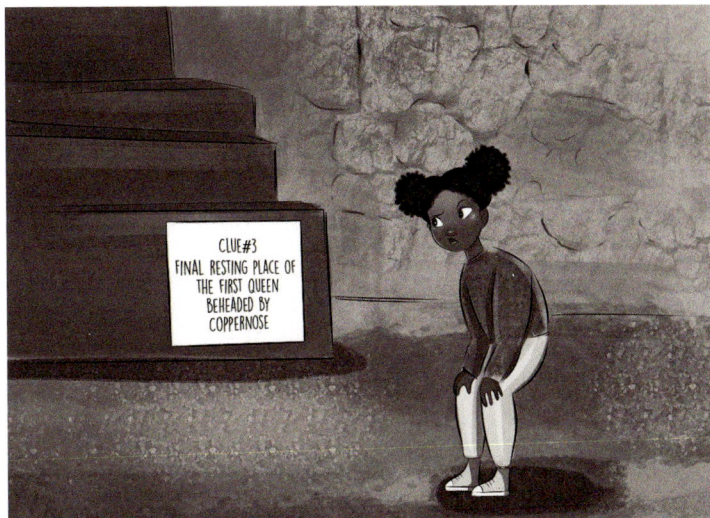

CLUE#3
FINAL RESTING PLACE OF
THE FIRST QUEEN
BEHEADED BY
COPPERNOSE

Amelia could tell that William was quickly beginning to regret his decision to hang out with her today.

"No!" said William firmly. "No, no, no! I'm going to turn around right now, head back to the library, lose myself in a good book and forget anything about this day ever happened!"

"William, *please*," said Amelia. "We can't come this far and then give up at the first hurdle. Anyway, I'm not asking you to come up with me. Just keep watch down here and make sure nobody sees me."

"What if you get caught?" asked William.

"That's where you come in," said Amelia. "Make a distraction. Pretend to see a shark in the Thames."

William rolled his eyes. "You're not serious, are you?"

"Please, William. I promise if there's nothing there we can go back to library and spend every single day there this summer."

"Fine," said William after a few long seconds of hesitation. "But hurry up."

---

18 **decision** choice – 18 **to hang out** to spend time together

Amelia smiled. "I'll be back before you know it!"

Amelia looked around the bridge. Because the second tower was closed, there were very few tourists standing by the door. Once she was certain nobody was looking at her, she stepped over the black and yellow tape and ran through the doorway.

Amelia's heart began to race as she hurried up the staircase. She was afraid that someone would suddenly appear and scold her for breaking into the tower, but mostly, Amelia was excited. She knew that William still wasn't convinced, but she was. She could feel it in her heart that something amazing was going to be waiting for her on the 201$^{st}$ step.

"198…199…200…201!"

The step looked like all the others. It was grey and made of stone. There was absolutely nothing special about it. Except…

Amelia crouched down and looked carefully at the corner of the step. There, carved in the stone, was a message.

Clue #2:

Clue #3: Final resting place of the first Queen beheaded by Coppernose.

Amelia reread the clue over and over until she had committed it to memory.

"The first Queen beheaded by *Coppernose*," Amelia muttered to herself as she walked back down the stairs. "*Coppernose*? Who is Coppernose?"

Amelia stomped angrily down the stairs. She had been right, there *was* a clue in the other Tower, but what good was that if she didn't understand what the clue meant? She had never even heard the name *Coppernose* before.

---

7 **to scold** to be angry – 16 **to carve** to write in the stone  – 22 **to behead** to cut sb's head off – 24 **to commit sth to memory** to learn sth

As she got to the bottom of the Tower, Amelia begun to hear what sounded like an angry conversation between two people. A tall man wearing a long, black trench coat was standing at the entrance to the glass floor bridge. A member of staff was standing in front of him, blocking the entrance to the Tower. Amelia could spot William standing a few feet away, anxiously peering through the doorway.

"…I'm sorry, sir," said the member of staff. "But as you can see, the Tower is currently closed for maintenance."

"I just need to check something. It'll take two minutes." said the man loudly. He tried to push pass the staff member, but she did not move.

"Sir," she said again. "I'm going to have to ask you to leave."

The man opened his mouth to argue, but the staff member began walking him away. Amelia could still hear the man begging to be let into the Tower as they walked back down the bridge. Once Amelia could not see or hear them anymore, she quickly walked through the doorway and ducked under the black and yellow tape.

"Finally!" William said with a sigh of relief. "I was getting worried. That man in the trench coat really wanted to go inside the Tower, but they wouldn't let him. I was scared that they'd find you and you'd get into big trouble."

Amelia hugged William. She didn't want to admit it out loud, but she had been a little worried too.

"Did you find the clue?" asked William. "Or can we finally go back to the library."

Amelia grinned. "I did find it! But I don't know what it means. What do you think? The next clue is in the *final resting place of the first Queen beheaded by Coppernose*. Any ideas?"

William scratched his chin and frowned. "Coppernose? Why does that sound familiar?"

3 **trench coat** a long coat that goes down to your knees – 6 **anxiously** nervously – 6 **to peer** to look – 18 **to duck under** to go under sth

Amelia shrugged.

William suddenly gasped and snapped his fingers together. "Coppernose! I remember I read a book all about The Tudors last year to help with that presentation we had to make for history class. It said that people called Henry VIII *Coppernose* because he made very cheap coins!"

"OK," said Amelia. "So, if Coppernose is Henry VIII, then we need to find the final resting place of the first Queen he beheaded. Wait! I've got it!" Amelia smiled widely. She had made a presentation about The Tudors last year too. It had been one of her favourite topics to learn about.

"Do you remember the rhyme Miss Smith taught us?" Amelia asked him. "Divorced, beheaded, died. Divorced, beheaded, survived! That's what Henry did to his six wives."

"But who was the first one he beheaded?"

"Anne Boleyn!" Amelia said loudly. "We need to go to the final resting place of Anne Boleyn. Do you know where that is?"

"It's in the Tower of London," said William. "I read about it in that book. Did you know Catherine Howard, Henry's fifth wife, is also buried there?"

Amelia wasn't listening. She was already running back down the bridge towards the exit.

"Come on William!" she yelled over her shoulder. "We've got to get to the Tower of London!"

Perhaps, if she hadn't been so excited and determined to find the next clue Amelia would have noticed something strange. As she and William ran down the bridge, the man in the long, black trench coat began to follow them.

---

25 **perhaps** maybe

Who is braver?
William or Amelia?

What did the man in
the trench coat want?

## Think about it...

William wants to go back to the library. Where
is your favourite place?

What do you know about Henry VIII?

# Chapter 4

The Tower of London was only a short walk away from Tower Bridge. If it had been any other day, Amelia would have stopped to admire the castle fortress, but that was the last thing on her mind today. All she cared about was finding the next clue. Amelia was also happy to see that William seemed excited too.

"The first message said we'd find plenty of jewels at the end of this treasure hunt!" William said excitedly as they queued up to enter the Tower of London. "Amelia, we might become millionaires!"

"We might become *billionaires*," Amelia said. "Aren't you glad we didn't go back to the library now?"

"Yes, yes, you were right," William laughed. "But we can't get too ahead of ourselves. We still need to find the next clue, and then the one after that.

"And then the one after that," Amelia agreed with a nod. "I hope there aren't too many clues. My parents said I have to be home by 8pm."

---

19 **fortress** walls around the castle – 22 **plenty of** lots of

When they got to the front of the queue, Amelia once again handed over some of the money her parents had given her. Her purse was beginning to feel quite light. Amelia hoped the other clues weren't in such expensive tourist attractions.

"I can't believe we're inside the Tower of London," William said in awe as they stepped through the black gates at the entrance. "I've been wanting my Dad to take me for ages, but he's always busy with work."

"Once we find the jewels we'll have enough money to come back as many times as you'd like," said Amelia. "But right now, we're on a mission."

"Right!" said William seriously. "We need to find out where Anne Boleyn is buried so we can find the next clue."

They walked around the grounds until they found a member of staff who helpfully told them that Anne Boleyn was buried in a chapel inside the grounds of the Tower of London. However, when they got to the chapel they discovered that it was only open to people who were part of a special tour group.

"Sorry kids," said the staff member who had helped them earlier. "Tour slots are all sold out for today so you won't be able to get into the chapel."

"We're getting into that chapel," Amelia muttered as soon as they staff member had walked away.

"How're we going to do that?" William asked. "It's not like at Tower Bridge where you just had to duck under some tape. If we're not part of a tour group, they won't let us in."

"That's why we're going to join a group," said Amelia. She had noticed something. Standing next to the entrance to the chapel were a group of people who all looked like tourists. In particular, there was a couple who looked like they were around Amelia's parents' age.

"Follow my lead," Amelia whispered to William.

---

16 **chapel** a small church – 18 **tour** a journey for pleasure to visit many different places

They walked quickly towards the group and stood casually next to the older looking couple. When the chapel doors opened and the tour guide told them they could come inside, nobody noticed Amelia and William walking in too.

Amelia and William didn't notice the man in the long, black trench coat either.

> Where was Anne Boleyn buried?

> How did William and Amelia get into the chapel?

## Think about it...

What would you do if you became a millionaire?

Amelia doesn't let anything stop her. Can you think of an example in your life where you didn't let something stop you?

---

1 **casually** in a relaxed and informal way

# Chapter 5

The chapel was much smaller than Amelia had imagined it would be. It was very beautiful but she could see it all from the entrance.

"Excuse me?" Amelia put her hand up high into the air and interrupted the tour guide. "Where is Anne Boleyn buried?"

"Anne Boleyn?" the tour guide asked. He looked confused. "Sorry, I'll get to her. I'm just giving you some history about the construction of the chapel. It's a very interesting story…"

Amelia stopped listening to the tour guide and looked around the chapel. She couldn't see anywhere in which it looked like Anne Boleyn might be. She saw a raised stone casket at the other end of the chapel. It seemed like the best place to start. While the tour guide pointed at some gold decorations on the wall, Amelia tried to sneak away from the group.

"Excuse me, miss," said the tour guide. "Can you stay over here with the group. You aren't allowed to wander in here."

---

20 **to interrupt** to speak when sb else is speaking – 26 **casket** a box for burying bodies – 28 **decoration** sth used to make a room like nicer – 29 **to sneak away** to get away without being seen – 31 **to wander** to walk around

"I just wanted to see Anne Boleyn," said Amelia. "Don't worry, I won't touch anything."

"That's not Anne Boleyn," said the tour guide. "If you listened to my explanation, you would know that that is the tomb of Sir Richard Cholmondeley, the man who built this tower."

Amelia was starting to get frustrated. "Then where is Anne Boleyn?" Was it possible that she and William had got the clue wrong? Maybe the clue wasn't talking about Anne Boleyn or Henry VIII? Maybe it was talking about someone else entirely?

"Miss," said the tour guide firmly. He sounded frustrated. "Can you please come back to the group? I promise you I'll show you Anne Boleyn's grave marker before we leave." As he said that, he pointed to the floor. Amelia glanced down. She couldn't believe she hadn't noticed before, but covering the marble floor were interesting carvings with names written around the edge. Written over the one nearest Amelia it said: *Queen Catherine Howard, 1541*.

Amelia gasped. "These are the grave markers?" she asked the tour guide. "So, Anne Boleyn has one in here too? Where is it?"

"Miss!" snapped the tour guide. "Please re-join the group otherwise I'll have to ask you to leave."

Reluctantly, Amelia walked back to the group. The tour guide glared at her as she fell back in line with William.

"Now we're finished with all these interruptions," said the tour guide. "Let me continue on with the history of the chapel."

The history of the chapel was interesting, but Amelia couldn't force herself to care about it. She was too focused on trying to find Anne Boleyn's grave marker. Every time she took one step away from the group, the tour guide yelled at her.

"Miss, you're on your final warning. If you step away from the group one last time, I'm going to have to ask you to leave."

---

14 **marble** a type of stone – 18 **grave marker** a sign to show who is buried there –
22 **reluctantly** without wanting to

So, Amelia waited patiently as the tour guide slowly walked them around the chapel, pointing out the grave markers for the others buried beneath the chapel. After what felt like much too long, the tour guide finally stopped at a marker in the middle of the chapel.

"And now we arrive at the main attraction," said the tour guide sarcastically as he looked at Amelia. "This is Queen Anne Boleyn's grave marker."

Amelia pushed to the front of the group and stared at the grave marker. It looked like all the other markers but Amelia knew there had to be something about it that set it apart from the rest. Once she was sure the tour guide wasn't paying her any attention – because he was too busy explaining the history behind one of the nearby paintings on the wall – Amelia crouched down to get a better look at the marker.

*There*! In the top right-hand corner of the marker, Amelia could make out a carving that didn't look like it belonged. She inched closer to the corner, only to find herself suddenly pulled backwards.

"Ouch!" Amelia yelled as the tour guide dragged her away from the marker. "What're you doing?"

He looked furious. "I told you many times, you aren't allowed to touch anything and you have to stick with the group. I'm afraid I'm going to have to ask you to leave."

"But—But—"

"Out!" yelled the tour guide. He opened the door to the chapel and pushed Amelia out of it. Before she even had the chance to turn around, he slammed the door shut behind him and Amelia was left outside.

∗∗∗

---

7 **sarcastically** meaning the opposite of what you say – 12 **to pay attention** to look at sb – 17 **to make out** to see sth with a little difficulty – 18 **to inch** to move forward a little bit

Almost 20 minutes later, the door to the chapel opened and William and the group came walking out. The tour guide walked past Amelia and glared at her. Amelia looked the other way and pretended not to see him.

"I'm so sorry, William," Amelia said as William approached her. "I've ruined everything for us. Now we won't be able to find the next clue."

To Amelia's surprise, William didn't look upset or angry with her. In fact, he looked quite happy. He had a big grin on his face and he kept hopping around from one foot to the other in excitement.

"You don't have to apologise," said William. He took a step closer to Amelia and whispered in her ear. "When the tour guide was kicking you out, I got a look at the marker!"

Amelia couldn't believe it. "You found the clue?"

William nodded. "Yes! But it doesn't make any sense. It's just a bunch of random letters."

"What was it?"

William opened his mouth to tell her, then suddenly closed it. A shadow loomed over them. Amelia and William turned around to find the man in the long, black trench coat standing behind them.

"Hello children," said the man.

---

17 **random** no order or reason to it

How does the tour guide feel about Amelia?

Why did it help that he threw Amelia out of the chapel?

## Think about it...

Amelia and William sneak into the chapel. Do you think that's OK? Why or why not?

# Chapter 6

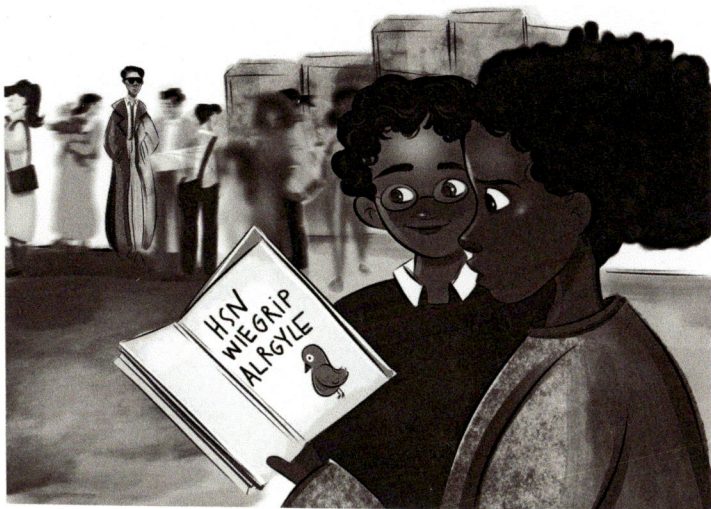

Amelia and William shared a nervous look between themselves. The man had a pointed face and was wearing big black sunglasses. He didn't look trustworthy.

"Our parents told us not to talk to strangers," said Amelia quickly.

The man laughed. It didn't sound like a real laugh at all. It sounded like the kind of laugh someone does when they're only pretending to find something funny.

"I just wanted to ask you a question," said the man. "I noticed you were very interested in Anne Boleyn's grave marker. Why was that?"

Amelia shrugged. "We're learning about her in school. I thought it was interesting."

William nodded in agreement.

The man looked at them for a few long seconds before he cleared his throat. "Very well then. Goodbye."

---

19 **trustworthy** sb you can believe – 20 **stranger** sb you don't know

Amelia and William watched as the man quickly walked away and disappeared into the crowds of tourists in the Tower of London.

"That was weird," said Amelia.

"Really weird," agreed William. "When I was looking at the grave marker, he was watching over my shoulder too."

"So strange," said Amelia. "But tell me, what was the clue?"

"Right!" said William. "Well, like I said, it didn't make any sense to me. It was just a bunch of letters." William pulled out a small notepad from his pocket and flipped it open. "I wrote it down because I knew I wouldn't remember them: HSNWIEGIRP ALRGYLE. And, even stranger, there was a carving of a small bird under the letters on the marker."

Amelia frowned. She asked William to repeat the letters to her a few more times. Then she slammed her fist into her palm.

"I've got it!" she shouted. "I think the letters have been scrambled to hide the message. Those kinds of puzzles are always in Dad's newspapers. Let me see your notepad for a minute."

William handed Amelia his notepad and watched as she began scribbling different letters across the page, trying to unscramble the clue.

"I think I've got it!" Amelia exclaimed after a few minutes had passed. "I think it says *Whispering Gallery*."

"Whispering Gallery?" repeated William. "Why does that sound familiar?" He thought about it for a few seconds before the answer came to him. "The bird!" William exclaimed. "Do you remember I said there was a bird underneath the letters?"

Amelia nodded.

"I think it was a wren. You know, like Christopher Wren?"

"He was the man who designed St. Paul's Cathedral, right?" Amelia asked. They had learned all about St. Paul's Cathedral in history class last year.

---

12 **carving** a drawing in stone – 17 **scrambled** in the wrong order – 20 **to scribble** to write quickly – 22 **to exclaim** to say sth loudly and with emotion

"Exactly," said William. "The Whispering Gallery must be inside St. Paul's Cathedral!"

"What are we waiting for?" asked Amelia. "Let's go!"

***

They had to take a bus to St. Paul's Cathedral. It didn't take very long, but Amelia and William were feeling excited and impatient.

"Why's it taking so long?" Amelia grumbled as the bus slowly crawled through the London traffic. "I wonder where the next clue will take us! What if—"

Amelia stopped talking. Standing a few feet away from them was the man who had spoken to them at The Tower of London. He was staring at them with an unpleasant look on his face.

"William!" Amelia hissed. "Look! It's that man."

"Oh yeah," said William. "Weird."

"Do you think he's following us?"

William snorted. "Definitely not. It's just a coincidence, don't worry about it."

Amelia frowned. She wasn't so sure that it was a coincidence at all.

How does the picture of the bird under the letters help them solve the puzzle?

Who do they see on the bus?

18 **coincidence** sth that happens without connection to sth else

## Think about it...

Amelia's parents told her not to speak to strangers. Why did they tell her that do you think?

Amelia and William feel impatient. When was the last time you felt impatient?

# Chapter 7

Amelia's purse was almost empty by the time she paid for their entry tickets into St. Paul's Cathedral.

"Don't worry about it," said William. "You'll get it all back once we find the treasure."

"Sure," said Amelia. She was feeling excited again. They ran into St. Paul's Cathedral and looked around in awe. It was *magnificent*.

Amelia had watched a documentary about the construction of St. Paul's Cathedral once, with her parents. It was nearly 100 metres tall and beautifully designed. Amelia gasped at the gold that lined the walls and the dome above them. She had never seen anything so stunning before. Their footsteps echoed as they walked through the cathedral.

"The Whispering Gallery is up there," said William. He pointed up at the circular dome above them. There was a walkway around

---

18 **cathedral** a very large and beautiful church – 28 **stunning** shockingly beautiful –
31 **walkway** a path for people to walk around

the inside of the dome for people to walk around and look down at the people below.

"Let's go!"

They followed the signs and the groups of tourists up the stone stairs to the top of the cathedral.

"Wow," said William once they arrived. "It's really high, isn't it?"

Amelia stepped towards the railings and peered over. The people below them looked like tiny ants. Amelia took a step back and shook her head. It was making her dizzy.

"Come on," said Amelia. "Let's find this next clue!"

They walked around the circular dome, looking closely at every inch of it to try and find something that seemed out of place.

"It looks like nobody's touched this place in years!" William said. He scrunched up his nose in disgust as he ran a finger over one of the metal bars and a cloud of dust puffed into his face. "How are we supposed to find the clue?"

"I don't know," said Amelia, "But keep looking." They couldn't give up now. Not when they were so close!

They walked about halfway around the dome when Amelia spotted something unusual. Tied around one of the metal bars was a bright red ribbon. It was very small, but it stood out against the dark metal walkway. Attached to the bottom of the ribbon, Amelia could see a small piece of paper.

"There!" she cried, pointing at the ribbon. "It's the clue!"

They ran towards the ribbon, but just as Amelia went to touch it, a large, gloved hand snatched it away.

Amelia and William looked up. Standing in front of them was the man from the Tower of London. He pulled his sunglasses down a little and glared at them.

"I believe this is mine," said the man. He ripped the small piece of paper off the bottom of the ribbon and put it in his pocket.

---

10 **dizzy** unbalanced – 12 **circular dome** circle shaped room

"Here's some advice, kids." He bent down and smirked at them.
"You got pretty far, I'll give you that, but this is dangerous work.
Leave the treasure hunting to the grown-ups. Or else."

"Or else, what?" said Amelia, suddenly feeling very brave. She
puffed out her chest and glared at the mystery man. "Give us back
our clue!"

"Or else, I might have to get rid of you myself."

Amelia looked over at William. He looked terrified.

"Right," said the man. "Now I've got what I need, I'll be going."
Without waiting for them to respond, the man quickly ran past
them and hurried back down the stairs.

***

"Now what do we do?" asked Amelia.

They had waited for a few minutes inside the cathedral to make
sure the mystery man was gone.

"What can we do?" said William, glumly. They walked out of
the cathedral and back into the summer sunlight. "He stole the
clue and you heard him. He'll hurt us if we keep looking."

Amelia laughed. "I'm not scared of him."

"Well, I am!" said William. "He looked very scary."

Amelia had to agree. The man did look scary. But she couldn't
believe their adventure was over. It wasn't fair. The man hadn't
solved all the clues before this one, *they* had. The man had just
followed them. They were the real treasure hunters, not him!

"Let's just go home," said Amelia. William was right. What else
could they do?

They started walking towards the bus stop when Amelia heard
a familiar voice. Standing at the bus stop was the man! He was on
the phone and didn't notice them.

---

3 **or else** sth might happen – 8 **terrified** very scared – 18 **glumly** unhappily – 30 **familiar**
sth you already know – 31 **to notice** to see

"Quick!" Amelia hissed. She pulled William into some bushes. They were hidden so the man couldn't see them, but they could hear him.

"…Got it boss!" said the man. "And I got rid of those silly kids too."

"Hey!" grumbled William. "We're not silly."

"Ssh!" said Amelia.

"…Yes, I know where the next clue is," continued the man. "Nelson's Column, that's right. Yes. Yes, boss. OK. Goodbye."

The man put his phone back into his pocket and waved to a passing black cab. Amelia and William watched as he climbed into it and quickly drove away.

"Did you hear that, William?" asked Amelia. She felt that familiar feeling of excitement begin to fill her up again. "They're heading to Nelson's Column!" She turned to William and grinned. "And so are we!"

How did the Whispering Gallery make Amelia feel?

How do Amelia and William find out about the next clue?

## Think about it…

Do your parents give you pocket money? What do you spend it on?

The man steals the clue from Amelia and William. Do you think this is fair?

# Chapter 8

Like the rest of London, Nelson's Column was incredibly busy when they arrived.

"At least this one's free," said Amelia. She didn't have much left from her summer spending money. If they didn't find the treasure, her parents would be furious!

Amelia had been to Nelson's Column before on a school trip a few years earlier. It was very tall and very thin. At the top of the stone column there was a statue of Admiral Horatio Nelson. The statue was too high up to see anything much, but Amelia remembered the pictures her teacher had shown her. Admiral Nelson wore a funny shaped hat and was holding a long sword. Amelia didn't think Admiral Nelson was the most interesting part about Nelson's Column. No, the most interesting part were the four bronze lions that surrounded the column. The lions were huge and sat there, permanently guarding the column.

"I don't see that man anywhere," said William.

---

17 **incredibly** very – 21 **furious** very angry – 31 **permanently** forever, always

Amelia nodded. She had been looking through the crowds of people too, trying to see if she could spot the man and his long trench coat.

"He must've come here already."

"That means he's already taken the clue!" said William sadly. "This was all a waste of time."

"Not necessarily," said Amelia. "Not all the clues were ones that could be taken like the one at St. Paul's Cathedral. The clue could still be here! We need to search. And we're going to start *there*," Amelia pointed at Nelson's Column. Something was calling her to it.

They ran over to the column and investigated the base. They couldn't find anything written on the stone steps or the bottom of the base of the column.

"There's nothing here!" whined William.

Amelia ignored him. She knew the clue was here somewhere, she just *knew* it. They hadn't come this far to turn away so soon.

"The clue must be higher up," decided Amelia. "We'll have to climb it. Here, give me a lift."

William didn't look pleased, but he didn't say anything as he helped Amelia climb up onto the column.

Amelia had just begun to peer around when a furious voice boomed out: "HEY YOU! STOP THAT, RIGHT NOW!"

Amelia fell off the column and on top of William.

"Ouch!" cried William.

"GET AWAY FROM THERE THIS INSTANCE!" yelled the voice.

Amelia and William looked up.

"Oh no," they said at the same time.

An angry looking police officer was walking towards them. They were in big trouble.

12 **to investigate** to search

What did Amelia find the most interesting part of Nelson's Column? Why?

Who told them to get off the column?

## Think about it...

Have you ever had a strong feeling about something? What was it about?

When was the last time you got in trouble?

# Chapter 9

"And what do you two think you're doing?" asked the police officer. He had his hands on his hips and was looking down at Amelia and William with a disappointed frown.

"We were just—" Amelia began, but the police officer continued talking.

"It's like nobody respects history anymore!" he yelled. "Do you know how long Nelson's Column has been here?"

Amelia shook her head.

"Since 1843!" said William. "I read about it in a book once."

"Exactly," said the police officer. "Since 1843! It's been here for hundreds of years so you two should have more respect for it! What if you damaged it by climbing it?"

Amelia suddenly felt bad. She hadn't thought about that. "I'm sorry," said Amelia. "You're right, we should respect history."

William nodded in agreement.

---

22 **to respect** to admire and care about sth

"Well," said the police officer. He looked a little less angry. "At least *you* apologised and seem polite. The man earlier didn't even listen to me."

Amelia's eyes went wide. "A man?"

"Yes," the police officer said with a scowl. "About ten minutes before you two arrived, a man in a trench coat was here trying to climb the column too! I couldn't believe it! I told him to get down, but he didn't listen, just kept climbing higher and higher. I was just about to radio the station to ask for some help, when he suddenly jumped down."

"Did he say anything?" Amelia asked. This could be what they were looking for!

"Not to me," said the police officer. "He ignored me, but he picked up his phone and started talking to someone. Kept saying they need to get to Westminster Palace! I told him that he wasn't going anywhere but the police station, but he didn't listen."

"Where did he go?" asked Amelia.

The police officer shrugged his shoulders. "I don't know, he just ran off. I assume he was heading to Westminster Palace."

Amelia smiled widely. "Thank you! Thank you!"

The police officer looked surprised. "Why're you thanki— Wait!"

Amelia grabbed William and began to run away. "We didn't find the clue, but the police officer gave us one anyway!" she said.

William looked just as excited as she did. "Westminster Palace!" he shouted. "Let's go!"

---

18 **to shrug your shoulders** to lift your shoulders up and down – 19 **to assume** to guess

Why was the police officer angry?

Where was the man going?

## Think about it...

Do you agree that we should have respect for history? Why?

Why is it important to apologise?

# Chapter 10

Amelia sighed sadly as she handed over the last remains of her summer spending money to the ticket attendant at the Palace of Westminster.

"That's it," said Amelia. "If this isn't the last clue, or the next location isn't free, this might be the end."

Amelia had never been to the Palace of Westminster before, but she'd seen it plenty of times when she and her family had travelled through London. She'd even seen the inside on the television before. They often showed clips of it during the evening news.

"Did you know that the King of England used to live here?" asked William as they walked through the building.

Amelia nodded. "Yes, my dad told me. He also told me that this isn't the original palace."

"That's right," said William. "It got destroyed a few times. There were two fires and it was hit by bombs in World War Two!"

---

24 **clip** short video

Amelia looked around the large building they were in. Suddenly, she couldn't help but think about all the history that surrounded them. The police officer was right. They had to respect it.

"We need to find the clue," said Amelia. "But we need to do it carefully. We don't want to break or damage anything."

"You're right," said William. "But where do we start?"

Amelia opened the map of the building the ticket attendant had given them. The Palace of Westminster was huge and there were many rooms and pathways to take. The clue could be anywhere! Amelia felt her hope begin to disappear. It would take them weeks to search every room in the palace, and they didn't have that time.

"Amelia!" William suddenly whispered. "Look!"

Amelia looked at where William was pointing. Standing opposite them, with his head buried in his own map of the building, was the man in the trench coat. Only this time, he wasn't alone. Another, shorter man, was standing beside him. The short man was also wearing a trench coat.

Amelia knew what to do.

"Let's follow them!"

They kept a few metres behind so they would not be noticed and follow the two men as they walked around the building. They walked all over the building but didn't stop anywhere.

"They look just as lost as us!" William said.

Amelia realised that he was right. The two men didn't know where the clue was either.

"We need to figure out what the clue they got from Nelson's Column was," said Amelia. "I'm going to try and get closer."

"Be careful," said William.

"I will," said Amelia. She crept closer to the two men, taking care to stay hidden in the shadows.

---

3 **to surround** to be everywhere around  – 31 **to creep** to move slowly and carefully

"…This is getting ridiculous," said the shorter man. "Where's the next clue?"

"I don't know!" snapped the taller man. "I can't figure it out either."

"Remind me, what was the clue again?"

"'*A gift from our friends down under…*'" said the taller man. "What does that mean?"

"I've got it!" yelled Amelia. She immediately gasped and put her hands over her mouth, but it was too late…

The two men turned to see Amelia standing near them.

The taller man's eyes opened wide. "You!" he shouted.

Amelia quickly turned around and ran. "Come on, William!" she shouted as she raced past him. "I know where the next clue is!"

William hurried after Amelia.

"Stop them!" the taller man yelled.

"Stop them right now!" the shorter man shouted.

Amelia and William ran all around the Palace of Westminster until the two men couldn't follow them anymore. They were too fast for them. When they finally stopped running, both Amelia and William were out of breath.

"I haven't run that fast in years," said William as he tried to catch his breath.

"Me neither," said Amelia. "But it'll be worth it, because I know where the next clue is!"

"Really?" said William.

"Yes," said Amelia with a grin. "Remember how you said the building was hit by bombs during World War Two?"

"Yes," said William. "They had to rebuild a lot of it."

"My dad told me that too," said Amelia. "And he also told me something else. The Speaker's chair was destroyed during the war too, so Australia send us a new one as a gift!"

---

3 **to snap** to say angrily

"OK…" said William. "But what does that have to do with the next clue?"

"I heard them talking about the last clue," Amelia told him. "It was '*A gift from our friends down under…*'. That must mean the chair!"

William smiled. "You're right! Let's go!"

> Why isn't Amelia happy?

> Why did Australia send Britain a new chair?

## Think about it…

Do you think William should have paid for the tickets?

What was the last gift you received? Who was it from?

# Chapter 11

The Speaker's Chair was in a room called The House of
Commons Chamber. It was the room Amelia had seen often on
the news. It was a long room, made almost entirely of wood and
filled with long, dark green chairs. At the very top end of the
room there was one large, green chair that stood out amongst the
rest. *The Speaker's Chair*.

"We have to be quick," said Amelia as they entered the
chamber. "I don't know where those two are hiding, but we don't
want them to catch us again."

"Agreed," said William.

They walked over to the Speaker's Chair and, when the other
tourists in the room had turned away, began looking for the clue.
There was nothing out of the ordinary on top of the chair, but
Amelia had a hunch…

"The clue was '*a gift from our friends down under*'," she
mumbled to herself. "Down under. That means Australia of
course, but what if it means something else too."

---

29 **out of the ordinary** different – 32 **to mumble** to speak quietly

**56**

"Like what?" asked William.

Amelia crouched down onto the floor and looked underneath the bottom of the chair. "Ahah! Like this!" she said happily. She reached under the chair and pulled out a small piece of paper that had been stuck to the bottom.

"It's the clue!" cheered William. "What does it say?"

Amelia read the clue:

Clue #6: Visit this bed, fit for a Queen, where the park without flowers and the park with plenty meet

"A park without flowers?" Amelia repeated as she read the clue again. "How is that possible? There's no such thing."

"But there is!" said William. He looked excited. "Do you remember that book I was reading at the library? The book about the history of London parks?"

Amelia rolled her eyes. Of course she remembered William's boring book. "What does that have to do with anything?"

"There was a special section about Green Park in the book," said William. "Green Park doesn't have any flowers! The story is, that long ago Queen Caroline got jealous because her husband, King George II, kept giving flowers to other women. So, she ordered that all the flower beds in Green Park be taken away! The 'park without flowers' must be Green Park!"

"Alright," said Amelia slowly. "So the first park is Green Park, but what about the second one?"

Amelia tried to think about everything she knew about Green Park and the parks around it. She'd been there many times with her family, and she was sure she'd seen flowers before. But where? *Where?*

"I know!" Amelia exclaimed. "St. James's Park! There are loads of flowers there. My parents and I walked through it to get to Buckingham Palace."

Amelia remembered her parents had taken her there so they could see the guards outside the palace. Amelia had a picture with her standing next to the guards, pretending to be one herself. She remembered something else about that trip.

"Right in front of Buckingham Palace, there's a bed of flowers near a statue created to honour Queen Victoria! And you can get to it by either walking through St. James's Park or Green Park. That bed is where the two parks meet! It must be there," said Amelia. "That's the only choice!"

"I think you might be right," said William. "Let's go!"

The two ran out of the room so fast, they didn't notice the two men from earlier hurrying after them.

> Why is Green Park known as the park without flowers?

> Which park near Buckingham Palace does have flowers?

## Think about it...

Do you think a park without flowers will be a nice place?

When was the last time you felt jealous?

6 **to honour** to show respect to sb

# Chapter 12

It only took 15 minutes to get from the Palace of Westminster to Green Park, but to Amelia it felt like forever.

"I can feel it," said Amelia as they waited for their bus to stop. "This is the final part of this treasure hunt, I just know it! We're going to find some treasure there."

Everything was leading up to this. They just had to make it to Green Park and find the flower bed from the clue.

"What are you going to spend your half on?" William asked.

"I'm definitely going to buy that new video game console," said Amelia. "But then I think I might go on a trip abroad. Maybe find some treasure in a new country," she laughed. "What about you?"

"I'm going to buy all the history books about London I can find!" said William. "I didn't know there was so much history in London."

"Me neither," said Amelia. "But it's all very interesting, isn't it?"

William nodded in agreement.

26 **trip abroad** holiday in a different country

When the bus stopped by Green Park station, Amelia and William jumped off it. Out of all the places they had been that day, Green Park was by far the busiest. There was an endless crowd of people walking towards the park. Amelia and William held onto each other's hands as they pushed through the crowd, so they didn't lose each other.

"We should walk through the park and head to Buckingham Palace," said Amelia. "The flower beds are just opposite the palace."

"Great idea," said William.

As they walked through the park, Amelia realised that William had been right. There were no flower beds in Green Park. There were little patches of yellow daffodils every so often, but it was clear they hadn't been intentionally planted. Green Park was nothing like the other parks in London filled with colourful flowers everywhere you turned. It was big and green, and beautiful in its own way.

"I wonder if that story about Queen Caroline and King George is true," said Amelia as they walked through the park. "Or do you think that someone just made it up one day?"

"I don't know," said William. "It's a funny story, but it's a sad one too. I feel sorry for Queen Caroline if it's true."

"Me too," said Amelia.

They continued on walking through the park without noticing that the two men were still following them.

\*\*\*

Buckingham Palace was even busier than Amelia had ever seen it before. The crowd outside the gates was so big, Amelia could barely see the guards standing outside.

---

14 **intentionally** on purpose

"Everyone wants to get a picture of the guards," William explained. "They look so cool, don't they?"

Amelia agreed. The guards at Buckingham Palace wore a bright red shirt, black trousers and a huge black, bearskin hat! It looked like a very warm hat, but the guards wore it even during the hottest weather. Amelia thought it was very impressive.

"We're not here to see the guards," Amelia said. "We've got our own mission!"

"Right," said William.

"See that," Amelia pointed at a circular area in front of Buckingham Palace. "That's the Queen Victoria Memorial. And those," she pointed just behind the memorial. "Those are the flower beds planted in honour of her. That's where the two parks meet! The treasure must be there!"

"But Amelia," said William slowly. "There aren't any flowers there."

William was right. The beds of flowers were there, but they were empty and only filled with dirt. The flowers hadn't bloomed yet.

"So?" asked Amelia. "The clue didn't say the flowers had to be there, just that it was a bed fit for a Queen. Where else could the treasure be?"

William thought about it for a few seconds, then shrugged. "You're right. We might as well have a look."

They pushed through the crowd and raced over to the flower beds. Most of them looked like they hadn't been touched in a while, but one bed looked like someone had recently dug it up.

"That one!" shouted Amelia. Her heart started to beat faster. This was it. They were almost there. "The treasure must be buried in that flower bed!" She took a step forward, but someone placed a hand on her shoulder and dragged her backwards.

---

11 **memorial** sth to remind people of a person or event – 18 **to bloom** to open (flowers) –
21 **fit for a Queen** perfect for a queen to use

Amelia looked up in horror. The tall man from before was staring down at her.

"Let me go!" yelled William. The short man was holding onto him too.

"Not so fast," said the tall man. "Well done for leading us here. We never would've guessed it if we hadn't followed you two."

Amelia scowled. They should have checked that they weren't being followed, but she was so excited she hadn't even thought about it.

"Leave us alone!" said Amelia. "This is our treasure. It's not our fault you weren't smart enough to find it yourselves."

The tall man growled at Amelia. "If we're not smart, how come we had you do all the hard work for us?"

"Yeah," said the short man. "Now all we have to do is grab the treasure. Sounds pretty smart to me."

They both laughed.

"Now," said the tall man. "Let's get rid of these two, then we'll come back and get the treasure." They started to pull Amelia and William away.

"Let us go!" shouted Amelia.

"Help! Help!" yelled William.

"Be quiet!" shouted the tall man.

"Shut up," yelled the short man.

"WHAT DO YOU THINK YOU'RE DOING TO THOSE CHILDREN?" roared a voice.

The two men were so shocked, they let go of Amelia and William. Standing in front of them all, with his hands on his hips, was the police officer from Nelson's Column.

"I had a funny feeling about you all," said the police officer. "So, I've been following you kids since you ran away. And it's a good thing I did!" He pointed at the two men. "Where were you taking those children?"

The men both looked nervous.

"We were just –" said the short man.

"Nothing, I mean we were only –" stammered the tall man.

"Well?" asked the police officer.

The two men looked at each other, then turned on their heels and ran as far as they could.

"Wait!" cried the police officer. "Stop!"

But it was too late. The two men had disappeared into the crowd.

Why were there some flowers in Green Park?

Who saves them from the two men?

## Think about it...

Are you more interested in history now?

William wants to buy history books.
What would you spend your treasure on?

# Chapter 13

*Now's my chance*, thought Amelia as she watched the police officer run into the crowd to try and find the two men.

"William, come on!" she yelled

The two ran towards the flower bed and dropped down onto their knees.

"Dig!" Amelia told him. "Dig as quickly as you can."

They dug their hands into the dirt and began digging as fast as they could. Amelia could see people start to notice them. People began telling them to stop. She could hear the police officer returning.

"What're you two doing? Get out of there!" shouted the police officer.

But Amelia didn't listen. She was so close! She dug and dug and dug until her fingers brushed against something hard. Amelia's heart pounded firmly in her chest as she wrapped her fingers around the item and pulled it out from the dirt.

---

31 **to pound** to hit hard and lots of times

"William," Amelia whispered as she stared at what she had pulled from the dirt. It was a small package, wrapped in an old kind of cloth. Amelia gently unwrapped the cloth and gasped. In her hands she was holding several small jewels. Some were diamonds, others were rubies, some were gold, and some were emerald and silver.

A crowd had begun to form around them. Everyone was silent as they stared at Amelia and William.

"William," said Amelia again. "William, we've done it! We've found the jewels!"

***

Amelia and William both smiled widely as the photographer took their picture. They had just finished being interviewed by a journalist for the biggest newspaper in the UK.

"This is the biggest story we've had in ages," said the journalist. "Two children found hidden jewels just outside Buckingham Palace! My editor isn't going to believe this."

"Well, it's the truth," said Amelia. "We found them. They're ours."

"Sorry children," said the police officer. He had introduced himself to Amelia and William as Terry. "But you can't keep those jewels."

"That's not fair," said William. "We're the ones who found them. It took us a lot of hard work too."

"I understand," said Terry. He put a hand on Amelia and William's shoulders and gave them a sad smile. "But the jewels don't belong to you. We don't know who they belong too. They might have been stolen! We're going to have to take them away to be investigated."

Amelia sighed. William was right, it wasn't fair, but she understood that it wasn't Terry's fault either.

"I guess I spent all my summer spending money for nothing," said Amelia sadly. Her parents weren't going to be happy with her.

"I'm sorry, Amelia," said William. He gave her a quick hug. "We tried our best."

"Hold on, hold on," said Terry with a smile. "Just because you can't keep the jewels, it doesn't mean that you won't get some kind of reward."

"A reward?" said Amelia brightly. "Money?"

Terry nodded. "I'm sure we can work something out. I'll talk to my boss and see what we can do."

"Yes!" Amelia and William both cheered. It wasn't the jewels, but it was something, and they were both quite happy about that.

"Terry," Amelia said suddenly. "What about the two men who were following us. Did you find them?"

Terry shook his head. "Sorry, but I lost them in the crowd. But I got a good look at them, so if they show up again I'll make sure to catch them. Now, let's get you two home."

> What did Amelia find after digging so hard?

> Why can't they keep the jewels?

## Think about it...

Do you think Amelia and William should be allowed to keep the jewels?

---

7 **reward** a gift for doing sth

# Chapter 14

## Three months later

Amelia and William were walking home from school together. It had been three months since their adventure in London together and they still couldn't quite believe everything that happened.

"It's a shame that we didn't get to keep the jewels," said William. "But at least we got some reward money."

They had each been give £200 from the police for their hard work in recovering the jewels. It was enough for Amelia to buy her new game console and have a little leftover to spend on snacks!

"Next time we'll just have to be more careful when we find the treasure," said Amelia.

"Next time?" squeaked William. "What do you mean next time?"

"There's lots of treasure out there, William," said Amelia with a grin. "And we're going to be the ones to find it!"

"Oh really?"

Amelia and William both turned around. Standing in front of them were the two men from their summer adventure.

"Don't look so alarmed," said the tall man. "We're not here to hurt you. My name is Lester, and this is Philip."

Philip, the short man, waved.

"What do you want?" snapped Amelia. "It's because of you that we lost the jewels."

"I know," said Lester. "I apologise for that. It was very unprofessional. That's why we've come to ask you if you'd like to join us."

"Join you?" asked William. "What's that supposed to mean."

"Your friend was right," said Philip. "There's a lot more treasure out there to find. That's why you should join us."

"We're members of a secret society called the Treasure Hunters," said Lester. "We travel all over the world looking for

---

31 **society** a club

hidden and lost treasure. We had been looking for those jewels for months, and you two found them in a day. You're clearly very talented."

Amelia and William both blushed.

"Our boss wants us to recruit you," said Lester. "What do you say?"

Amelia and William looked at each other and grinned.

"Yes," said Amelia. "We'll do it!"

What was their reward?

What does Lester's boss want?

## Think about it…

Would you like to search for hidden treasure?

3 **talented** good at what you do

# Activities

# Focus on the story

## 1. True or false?

Are these sentences true or false? Write the correct answers in your notebook.

|  | | True | False |
|---|---|:---:|:---:|
| 1. | Amelia and William found the first clue in a bookshop. | ☐ | ☐ |
| 2. | Tower Bridge was empty. | ☐ | ☐ |
| 3. | William didn't want to sneak into the next tower. | ☐ | ☐ |
| 4. | Henry VIII divorced Anne Boleyn. | ☐ | ☐ |
| 5. | William has never been to the Tower of London before. | ☐ | ☐ |
| 6. | Amelia and William joined a school group to get into the chapel. | ☐ | ☐ |
| 7. | A wren is a type of bird. | ☐ | ☐ |
| 8. | Amelia read the clue at St. Paul's Cathedral. | ☐ | ☐ |
| 9. | There were four lions at Nelson's Column. | ☐ | ☐ |
| 10. | They found the next clue at Nelson's Column. | ☐ | ☐ |
| 11. | Amelia still had some money after paying for their tickets at the Palace of Westminster. | ☐ | ☐ |
| 12. | America gave the UK the Speaker's Chair as a gift. | ☐ | ☐ |
| 13. | There are no flower beds in Green Park. | ☐ | ☐ |
| 14. | The two men let Amelia and William find the treasure. | ☐ | ☐ |
| 15. | Amelia and William kept the jewels. | ☐ | ☐ |

## 2. What happened where?

Match the place to what happened there.

| | |
|---|---|
| 1. The library | a. They go to the wrong tower. |
| 2. Tower Bridge | b. The man steals the clue first. |
| 3. Tower of London | c. A journalist interviews them. |
| 4. St. Paul's Cathedral | d. They get stopped by the police. |
| 5. Nelson's Column | e. Amelia finds the first clue. |
| 6. Palace of Westminster | f. They find the Speaker's Chair. |
| 7. Buckingham Palace | g. Amelia gets kicked out of the chapel. |

## 3. What does each character want to do?

Fill in the gap with the correct character name.

| Lester | Amelia | Terry | William | Lester's boss |
|---|---|---|---|---|

1. _____ wants to find all the clues and find the hidden treasure.
2. _____ wants people to stop climbing on Nelson's Column.
3. _____ wants to stop the children and find the treasure himself.
4. _____ wants to go back to the library and read a book.
5. _____ wants to invite Amelia and William to join the Treasure Hunters.

## Focus on the people

### 1. What are Amelia and William like?

Put the words in the box under the right column. Some words can be used for both characters. Add any more words you think describe Amelia and William.

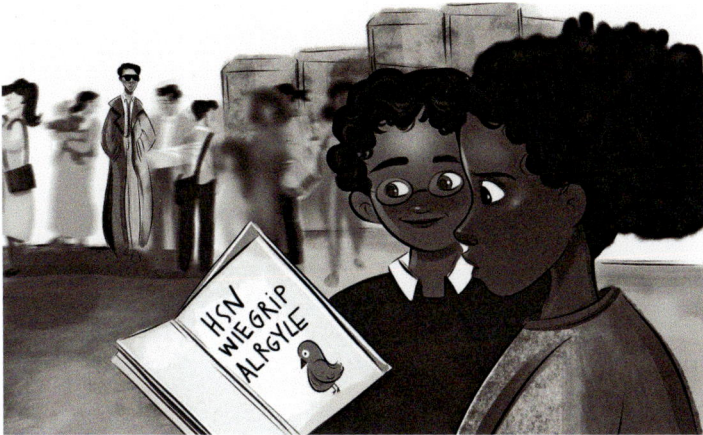

| worried | nervous | smart | brave |
|---|---|---|---|
| determined | adventurous | quick thinking | excitable |

| | | |
|---|---|---|
| Amelia  |  | William |
| | | |

# Focus on grammar

## 1. Which word works?

Choose the correct words from the box to complete the question.
Then answer the question in your notebook.

| who | what | how many | where | while | why |
|-----|------|----------|-------|-------|-----|

1. _____ many steps are in the towers of Tower Bridge?
2. _____ did people call Henry VIII Coppernose?
3. _____ was attached to the ribbon in St. Paul's Cathedral?
4. _____ stopped Amelia and William from climbing on Nelson's Column?
5. _____ did Amelia and William go after Nelson's Column?

## 2. What's the correct form?

Complete these sentences with the correct form of verb.

1. Amelia _____ (flick) through the pages of the book.
2. She ignored William and _____ (run) ahead.
3. The man climbed into the black cab and quickly _____ (drive) away.
4. William helped Amelia _____ (climb) onto the column.
5. She had _____ (saw) the Palace of Westminster on TV before.
6. Amelia and William _____ (dig) their hands into the dirt.

# Build your vocabulary

# Focus on words

**1. Write the word correctly in your notebook and then match the word with the right definition.**

| | |
|---|---|
| 1. sytemry | a. to believe in something |
| 2. tcocontnisur | b. very amazing and beautiful |
| 3. nneocicvd | c. a small church |
| 4. eeuuq | d. something that is difficult to understand or explain |
| 5. atnegfnciim | e. line |
| 6. oaeogspli | f. someone you can trust |
| 7. acehlp | g. the building of something |
| 8. rotsrtthwuy | h. a formal way of saying sorry |

**2. Complete the sentences in your notebook with the correct words from the box.**

| | | | |
|---|---|---|---|
| society | respect | notice | carving |
| coincidence | trip abroad | strangers | terrified |

1. Amelia's parents told her not to talk to _____.
2. William noticed a _____ of a small bird by Anne Boleyn's grave marker.
3. It wasn't a _____ at all.
4. The man scared William so much, he was _____.
5. Amelia and William didn't _____ the man following them.
6. It's important to _____ history!
7. Amelia wanted to spend her money on a _____.
8. Lester and Philip asked Amelia and William to join their secret _____.

# The Hidden Jewels of London – the mind map

Make your own mind map of words connected to the story.
Think of words to add to each topic area. You can add your own
topic areas too.

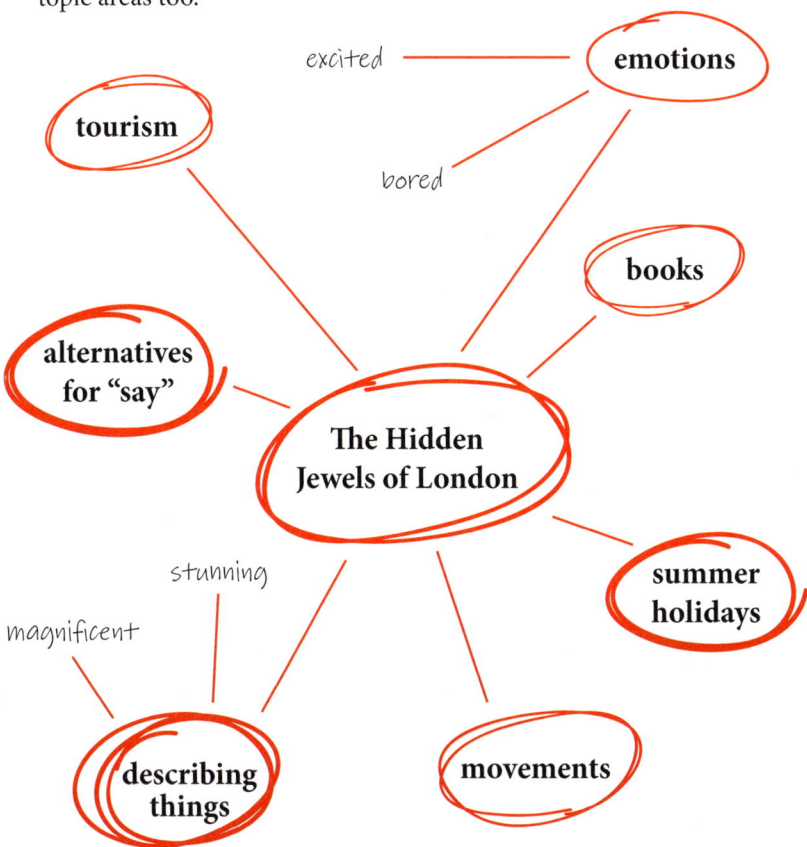

excited — emotions

tourism

bored

books

alternatives for "say"

The Hidden Jewels of London

magnificent

stunning

describing things

movements

summer holidays

Compare your words with the words on the next pages. Did you
include some of the same words? Tick the words you know and
look back at the text and explanations to check the meanings of
any new words. You can add your own words and notes to the
glossary like the examples.

# Glossary

| | New word? | Notes / connected words |
|---|---|---|

**Summer holidays**

hang out with friends ☐

reading ☐

spending money ☐

solve puzzles ☐

treasure hunt ☐

**Books**

adventure ☐

detective ☐

encyclopedia ☐

history ☐

library ☐

mystery ☐

**Tourism**

crowds ☐

entry ticket ☐

queue ☐

ticket attendant ☐

ticket office ☐

tour guard ☐

tourist attraction ☐

**Emotions**

angry ☐

anxious ☐

bored ☐

confused ☐

excited ☐

glum ☐

|  | New word? | Notes / connected words |
|---|---|---|
| happy | ☐ | |
| impatient | ☐ | |
| nervous | ☐ | |
| terrified | ☐ | |
| upset | ☐ | |
| worried | ☐ | |

## Movements

| bump | ☐ |
| crouch | ☐ |
| dig | ☐ |
| drag | ☐ |
| duck | ☐ |
| flick | ☐ |
| hug | ☐ |
| kneel | ☐ |
| ran | ☐ |
| roll | ☐ |
| snap | ☐ |
| walk | ☐ |
| wave | ☐ |

## Describing things

| amazing | ☐ |
| beautiful | ☐ |
| colourful | ☐ |
| cool | ☐ |
| magnificent | ☐ |
| new | ☐ |
| old | ☐ |
| small | ☐ |
| stunning | ☐ |

|  | **New word?** | **Notes / connected words** |
|---|---|---|
| **Alternatives for 'say'** | | |
| ask | ☐ | |
| boom | ☐ | |
| cheer | ☐ | |
| exclaim | ☐ | |
| growl | ☐ | |
| hiss | ☐ | |
| laugh | ☐ | |
| mumble | ☐ | |
| pant | ☐ | |
| roar | ☐ | |
| shout | ☐ | |
| sigh | ☐ | |
| wheeze | ☐ | |
| whine | ☐ | |
| whisper | ☐ | |
| yell | ☐ | |

🌐 **Find out more**

1. Choose one of the locations Amelia and William visited in the story. Research it and make a short presentation about it.

2. Find five more tourist attractions in London. Write down at least one interesting fact about each one.

| Tourist attraction | An interesting fact |
|---|---|
|  |  |
|  |  |
|  |  |
|  |  |
|  |  |

3. What do you know about the guards at Buckingham Palace? Write down three interesting facts.

1. _____
2. _____
3. _____

4. Imagine you are the journalist who interviews Amelia and William. Write your own newspaper article about their adventure!

# Answer key

# Focus on the story

## Questions at the end of each chapter

### Chapter 1
- mystery books
- non-fiction books

### Chapter 2
- buy a video console
- Amelia

### Chapter 3
- Amelia
- to go inside the Tower

### Chapter 4
- in a chapel inside the grounds of the Tower of London
- They stood next to a couple who looks as though they could be their parents.

### Chapter 5
- She makes him angry and frustrated.
- It gave William an opportunity to look at the marker.

### Chapter 6
- A **wren** is a bird. The Whispering Gallery is in St. Paul's Cathedral. Christopher **Wren** designed St. Paul's Cathedral.

### Chapter 7
- dizzy
- They listened to the man on the phone.

## Chapter 8
- The lions. They were always guarding the column.
- an angry police officer

## Chapter 9
- because they weren't showing any respect for history
- to Westminster Palace

## Chapter 10
- because she now has no money
- because the original one was destroyed in the war

## Chapter 11
- Queen Caroline didn't like it when her husband gave flowers to other women, and ordered that all flowers in Green Park be taken away.
- St. James's Park

## Chapter 12
- because they hadn't been planted intentionally
- the police officer from Nelson's Column

## Chapter 13
- the jewels – diamonds, rubies, gold, emeralds, silver
- because they don't belong to them

## Chapter 14
- £200 each
- for him to recruit the children

1. 1. E, 2. A, 3. G, 4. B, 5. D, 6. F, 7. C
2. 1. False. Amelia and William found the first clue in a library.
   2. False. Tower Bridge was filled with tourists.
   3. True
   4. False. Henry VIII had Anne Boleyn beheaded.
   5. True
   6. False. They stood next to an older looking couple.
   7. True
   8. False. The man took the clue first.
   9. True.
   10. False. They can't find the clue.
   11. False. Amelia handed over the last of her summer spending money at the Palace of Westminster.
   12. False. Australia gave the UK the Speaker's Chair as a gift.
   13. True
   14. False. They tried to stop them.
   15. False. Amelia and William had to give the jewels to the police.
5. Lester's boss

# Focus on the people

1. 1. Amelia, 2. Terry, 3. Lester, 4. William, 5. Lester's boss

# Focus on grammar

1. 1. How many / 206 steps
   2. Why / Because he made very cheap coins.
   3. What / A small piece of paper.
   4. Who/ The police officer did.
   5. Where / Palace of Westminster
2. 1. flicked, 2. ran, 3. drove, 4. climb, 5. seen, 6. dug

# Focus on words

1. 1. mystery; D, 2. construction; G, 3. convinced; A, 4. queue; E, 5. magnificent; B, 6. apologies; H, 7. chapel; C, 8. trustworthy; F
2. 1. strangers, 2. carving, 3. coincidence, 4. terrified, 5. notice, 6. respect, 7. trip abroad, 8. society

Now do the quizzes!